SPORTING SKILLS

RUGBY

CLIVE GIFFORD

Published in paperback in 2014

Wayland
Hachette Children's Books
338 Euston Road
London NW1 3BH

Wayland Australia
Level 17/207 Kent Street
Sydney, NSW 2000

Managing Editor: Rasha Elsaeed
Produced by Tall Tree Ltd
Editor: Jon Richards
Designer: Ben Ruocco
Photographer: Michael Wicks
Consultant: Tony Buchanan

British Library Cataloguing in Publication Data

Gifford, Clive
  Rugby. – (Sporting skills)
  1. Rugby football – Juvenile literature
  I. Title
  796.3'33

ISBN 9780750281201
      796.333
Printed in China

10 9 8 7 6 5 4 3 2 1

Wayland is a division of Hachette Children's Books, an Hachette Livre UK company.
www.hachette.co.uk

Picture credits
All photographs taken by Michael Wicks, except;
Cover Dreamstime.com/Patrick Breig,
5 Howard Burditt/Reuters/Corbis

Acknowledgements
The author and publisher would like to thank the following people for their help and participation in this book:
Old Albanian RFC and Neil Dekker

The website addresses (URLs) included in this book were valid at the time of going to press. However, because of the nature of the Internet, it is possible that some addresses may have changed, or sites may have changed or closed down since publication. While the author and Publisher regret any inconvenience this may cause the readers, no responsibility for any such changes can be accepted by either the author or the Publisher.

Disclaimer
In preparation of this book, all due care has been exercised with regard to the advice, activities and techniques depicted. The publishers regret that they can accept no liability for any loss or injury sustained. When learning a new sport it is important to get expert tuition and to follow a manufacturer's instructions.

CONTENTS

WHAT IS RUGBY?

Rugby union is a powerful and very skilful 15-a-side team sport where players can kick, pass or run with an oval-shaped ball on a large grass pitch. It demands players work hard together as a team and it is a sport played in dozens of countries around the world by men and women, girls and boys.

POINTS SCORING

A team with the ball tries to advance up the pitch while the team without the ball attempts to stop the attacking team by defending. At each end of the pitch is an in-goal area. Teams attempt to score a try worth five points by grounding the ball in an opponent's in-goal area. If a try is scored, the team gets a kick at the goalposts for a further two points, called a conversion. Penalty kicks awarded by the referee are worth three points if scored, as are drop kicks, which are kicks taken at the goal in open play.

STARTING OUT

For young players who are just starting to play rugby, there are a number of scaled-down versions of the sport played on smaller pitches and with modified and simpler laws. Most of these versions of the game concentrate on running, passing and catching the ball and allow little or no contact. Tag rugby, for instance, replaces real tackling with defenders trying to grab and remove tags attached to the players' clothing. Once the tag is removed by a defender, the player with the ball is considered tackled and has to stand still and pass the ball.

A full-sized rugby ball is approximately 30 centimetres (12 inches) long and weighs up to 440 grams (1 pound). Smaller, lighter versions of the ball are made for junior players.

A full game of rugby union is split into two halves, each lasting 40 minutes and is started with a kick-off from the halfway line. The kick-off must travel at least 10 metres (33 feet) forwards.

At each end of a pitch in the middle of the try line is a set of goalposts. The two uprights are 5.6 metres (19 feet) apart and often covered in protective padding around their bases. The crossbar runs between the uprights 3 metres (10 feet) off the ground.

RUGBY LEAGUE AND RUGBY SEVENS

There are various forms of rugby, each played under a different set of laws. Rugby league developed when a group of rugby clubs from northern England split away in the 1890s. It is now a popular sport in Britain, France, Australia and New Zealand with 13 players a side, quick ways of restarting the game and four points for a try. Rugby sevens is a dynamic and exciting version of rugby union, played in short bursts by seven players a side on a full-sized rugby pitch. This book will look at the skills and techniques needed to play rugby union.

Jason Robinson of England breaks clear of French defenders during the semi-final of the 2007 World Cup.

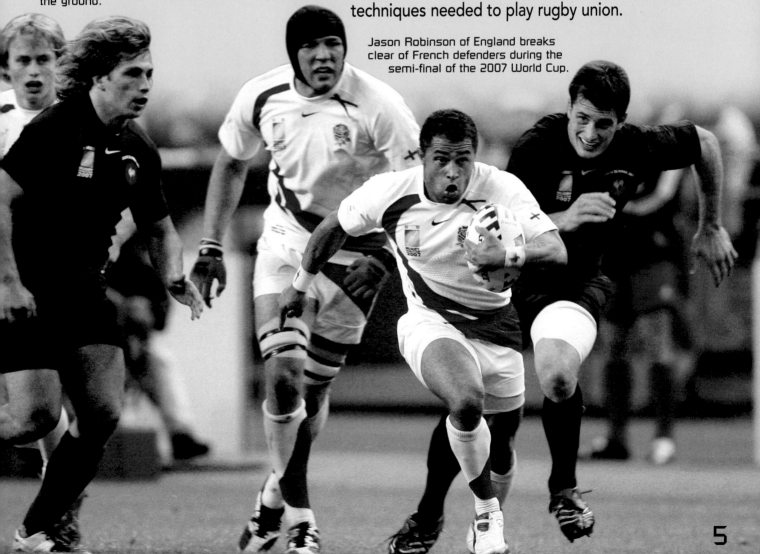

THE PLAYERS AND PITCH

A rugby team is split into two groups; forwards and backs. The eight forwards form scrums and contest lineouts (see page 24). The seven backs feature in attacks but also perform defensive duties. Two of the backs, the scrum-half (number nine) and the fly-half (number ten), usually link play between the forwards and the backs.

PLAYER PREPARATION

Different positions require different skills. Forwards who compete in the lineout, for example, need to be tall and good jumpers, while in the backs, the two wingers need to be fast runners. All players, though, need to be skilled in attack and defence. They must also work on their strength, fitness, pace and stamina – the ability to work hard for long periods. Junior players, especially, should concentrate on the basic skills, such as passing, receiving and general ball-handling. They should also work hard at set piece skills, such as the lineout and team defence.

Rugby boots

Rugby boots come in many designs, but most feature screw-in studs to provide grip. Many are cut higher than football boots and give more support to a player's ankles. Make sure that your boots are comfortable and fit well, and that they are clean and dry after each match. Always check that the studs are screwed in tightly.

This player is wearing typical rugby kit over a close-fitting undershirt to keep warm during training. Rugby shirts and shorts are made of hard-wearing cotton. Keep your shirt tucked into your shorts as this gives opponents less to grab hold of. Long socks are held up with tape or elastic and cover up shinpads, which some players wear to protect the bony parts of your lower legs.

THE PITCH

A rugby pitch measures about 100 metres (330 feet) long and up to 69 metres (230 feet) wide. At each end of the pitch is an in-goal area measuring up to 25 metres (83 feet) deep. The front of the in-goal area is marked by the try line and the back by the dead-ball line. The touchlines that mark the edge of the pitch are considered out of play. If the ball or a player holding the ball touches one of these, for example, then the ball is in touch and out of play and a lineout is awarded to the other team.

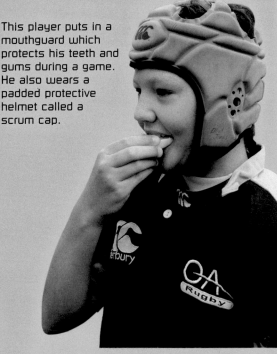

This player puts in a mouthguard which protects his teeth and gums during a game. He also wears a padded protective helmet called a scrum cap.

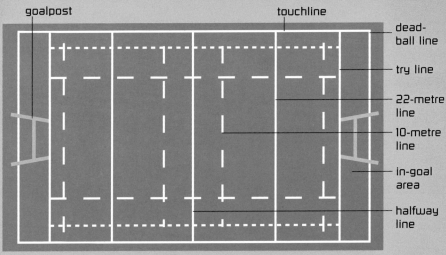

goalpost   touchline

dead-ball line
try line
22-metre line
10-metre line
in-goal area
halfway line

A typical rugby pitch with its markings. The 22-metre line is used for 22-metre drop outs, while the dashed lines running parallel with the sidelines, 5 metres (17 feet) and 15 metres (50 feet) in, are used to help judge the positioning of lineouts.

This coach works with his players on a passing drill. A coach teaches and improves players' skills as well as getting them to work well as a unit.

A group of players warm up before a training session. Whether training or playing a match, rugby union puts lots of strain on your body. A warm-up session loosens muscles and gets the blood pumping round your body.

A group of forwards have secured the ball. The scrum-half links play by picking up the ball and making a pass to one of his backs who may choose to kick, run or pass the ball.

THE REFEREE AND LAWS

The laws of rugby union are complex in places, but your coach can help explain anything you find puzzling. Knowing the laws well is essential as it allows you to exploit your skills to the maximum and avoid giving away costly penalties.

MATCH OFFICIALS

A rugby match is run by a referee and two touch judges who patrol the touchlines during the game. When a kick on goal takes place, the two touch judges stand behind the posts and signal with their flags whether the kick was successful or not. The touch judges also help the referee decide which side should get the ball when it leaves the pitch and will also advise the referee of any foul play they spot during the game.

The referee must be aware of many different laws during a match, from when a try is scored to whether the ball has been thrown forwards or knocked on. He is also responsible for starting and stopping the game with a whistle. If there has been foul or dangerous play, the referee may send off a player for ten minutes (the sin bin) or, for the most serious offences, send a player off the pitch permanently.

The player carrying the ball has been tackled and then pushed over the sideline and into touch by an opponent. Providing the tackling is legal and not dangerous, the referee will award the lineout to the tackling player's team because a member of the attacking side carried the ball off the pitch.

Referee signals

Referees have a number of signals which they use to communicate decisions to the teams and spectators.

The referee's signal here indicates that a try has been scored.

The referee's signal here indicates a scrum.

The referee's signal here indicates obstruction.

The referee's signal here indicates that a penalty has been given.

The referee's signal here indicates a free kick has been given.

PENALTY OFFENCES

A referee awards a penalty to one team when the other team has been guilty of one of a number of offences. These include obstructing members of the other side by unfairly blocking their path, tackling a player without the ball, tripping an opponent and causing a scrum or maul (see page 23) to collapse.

PENALTY OPTIONS

When a penalty is awarded, players have a number of choices. They can kick the ball to touch and get the throw in at the lineout. Alternatively, they can ask for a scrum to be set with them getting the put-in (see page 26), take a tap penalty (see right) or they could take a penalty kick on goal which, if successful, is worth three points (see page 28).

Tap penalty

1 This player has chosen to take a tap penalty. He must tap the ball with his foot and get it under control in his hands without knocking the ball forwards.

2 The player can now run, kick or pass. If he runs, opponents who were not 10 metres (33 feet) back when he took the penalty cannot tackle him until he has run 10 metres (33 feet) forwards.

This player is restarting a game with a 22-metre drop out, drop-kicking the ball from just inside his 22-metre area. A 22-metre drop out is awarded when a player touches the ball down in his or her own in-goal area after the opposition has kicked the ball over the try line.

9

PASSING AND RECEIVING

Passing is the most basic skill in the game and it should always be backwards or sideways, never forwards. It allows a team to move the ball around the pitch, and so keep possession and look for opportunities to attack. Many of the passes you make in a game will use the sideways, or lateral, pass technique but the pop pass is also useful in contact situations.

PASSING TECHNIQUE

Beyond the basic technique used in passing, players need to develop other skills to make their passing as crisp, accurate and decisive as possible. This comes with hours of practice and with experience in game and contact situations against opponents. As a passer on the move, you must be as aware of your receiver as possible. You will have to judge the speed of the receiver and the direction in which he or she is running. In effect, you have to pass to where they will be when the pass reaches them and not where they are when you let go of the ball.

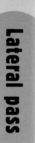 **Lateral pass**

1 These players are practising the lateral pass by passing in a line. The player on the left is about to receive the ball.

2 The receiver keeps his eyes on the ball. He holds his hands out with his fingers wide open, ready to catch the ball.

3 The receiver then turns his head to face the target of his pass. He holds the ball between waist and chest height and must judge the angle and distance of the pass he is about to make.

4 He swings his arms across his body and aims the ball in front of the next receiver. He flicks his wrists and fingers as the ball leaves his hands, which follow through and point at the target.

PASSING TIPS

You need to judge the right amount of force to put into your pass. For longer passes, players tend to turn more sharply at the waist to get a longer, more powerful swing of the arms. However, too much force in a pass to a receiver nearby can result in the ball missing them or a fumble, which could lead to the other side gaining possession. Finally, a crucial part of attacking is timing the pass so that it puts your team-mate into a better position than you.

A good grip of the ball for passing sees the ball held in your hands lengthways with the fingers pointing along the ball's length.

Both the passer and the receiver have their eyes on the ball and their arms and fingers outstretched as the ball has left the passer and is about to be gathered cleanly by the receiver.

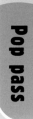
Pop pass

1 In a match, the aim of passing is to get past defenders and to get a team-mate into a good position. Here, the passer has decided to delay his pass to help put his team-mate in a better position.

2 He plans to make a short pop pass, which is performed using the same technique as the lateral pass but with a shorter swing.

3 Timing is the key to this pass. The passer waits until the defender is committed to tackling him before releasing the ball.

4 The passer releases the ball at a slight upwards angle to 'pop' the ball up at a nice height for the receiver to catch easily and sprint away.

CATCHING AND HANDLING

Catching the ball from a pass is only one way of handling the ball. During a match, the ball can come to a player at all heights and angles. A good player knows the skills involved in taking the ball from a range of positions and gathering it in securely.

TIPS FOR RECEIVING

When looking to receive the ball from a pass or an opponent's kick, you must stay alert and aware and keep watching the ball. Many dropped catches and knock-ons occur when players take their eyes off the ball. A knock-on is when a player drops the ball and knocks it forwards. A poor pass or catching attempt that creates a knock-on results in the referee awarding a scrum to the other side.

If you are in your own 22-metre area as you try to catch a kick, you can call a mark. This means shouting 'mark' loudly as you catch the ball. If successful, the referee will award you a free kick.

Standing catch

1 This player has got under a kick and looks to catch it from a standing position. He watches the ball with his arms raised and his elbows bent.

2 With his fingers spread, the player reaches up and gathers in the ball. He brings the ball into his chest to slow it down on impact.

3 The catcher's knees bend and his hips sink as he folds his body around the ball. This can help to cushion the ball as well as protecting it from opponents.

1 This player has chosen to jump to take a catch. He leaps up with his arms high and eyes on the ball.

2 The player catches the ball in mid-air and pulls it into his chest. The opposition cannot tackle him while he is the air.

3 The catcher turns on landing to protect the ball. This also means that if the ball is fumbled, it is likely to travel backwards.

Collecting a ball rolling on the ground calls for great concentration as the ball could bobble or alter its path. This player bends his legs with his body in line with the ball and his fingers spread to scoop it up.

BALL HANDLING

Getting a really good feel for the ball is important as it will enable you to not only catch the ball at regular heights but also to handle the ball when it is rolling along the ground or flying through the air at an unexpected angle. Coaches encourage ball handling through many different drills and fun games. Passing the ball around your body or throwing the ball up and just over your shoulder and twisting at the waist to catch it are two simple examples.

1 An alternative way to gather a rolling ball safely is the slide method. The player sprints hard to get to the ball first.

2 He drops to the floor and slides as he gets his hands on the ball. If he fumbles, his direction will take the ball backwards and not forwards, so avoiding a knock-on.

3 With the ball under control, the player rolls over to face forwards. He looks to get to his feet as quickly as possible.

KICKING FOR POSITION

All players should know how to perform kicks into touch as well as attacking kicks, such as the grubber. A loose ball on the floor can also see footballing skills come into play as an attacker tries to kick the ball forwards and then pick it up or, if it goes over the try line, to drop onto it to score a try.

The kicker releases the ball so that it is almost flat but pointing down a little at the front and slightly angled. The ball should reach the top of your foot at the same angle as it leaves the hands.

Touch kick

1 This player has just caught the ball and decides to make a quick, long kick with his right foot, aiming for the ball to cross the touchline.

2 He moves the ball in his hands as he starts to swing his left foot forwards to take a step. Once the left foot is planted, he gets his weight over that foot with his head down and eyes on the ball.

3 The ball is dropped and not thrown into the air, so that it is at the right angle when it makes contact with the boot. The right leg swings through with the ankle stretched and toes pointed.

POSITION AND SAFETY

Kicking the ball in open play usually gives possession to the opposition. When a side is deep in its own half and under pressure, gaining territory at the expense of giving away possession is often considered acceptable. Players look to kick as long as possible so that their forwards can contest a lineout farther up the pitch. From behind the 22-metre line, the ball can be kicked out on the full (without bouncing on the pitch). Outside the 22-metre area, players must aim their kicks to bounce before going out over the touchlines, otherwise the referee will bring play back to where the kick was made and award a lineout to the other side.

4 The foot strikes the ball on the boot laces. Good timing and a long swing of your foot will guarantee a good kick.

ATTACKING KICKS

Some kicks are used in attack to outwit an opposition defence. These include a high, hanging kick in difficult conditions, targeting opposition backs who are not good at catching a high ball. With a defence rushing up to face you and your team-mates, a grubber kick along the ground and behind the defence, or a short chip over the heads of the defenders can offer an excellent opportunity for you or a team-mate to run onto and collect the ball.

A high, hanging kick can give your team-mates time to chase and put opponents under pressure. The kick is similar in technique to the touch kick but the ball is held and dropped vertically. The ball is kicked through its centre and the kicker's foot follows through as high as possible.

1 The grubber kick can be handy when faced with little space to move and an approaching defence. The ball is held in both hands one either side and released around or below waist height.

2 The player gets his body weight over the ball and swings his lower leg back and forwards at the knee. Connection is made with the boot laces just above the middle of the ball as it reaches the ground.

Grubber kick

3 The player tries to keep his foot pointed and his follow-through low. As a result, the ball should travel along the ground, end over end.

RUNNING WITH THE BALL

Because a ball can only be passed backwards or sideways, players have to run with the ball to move it forwards and to keep possession. Players need good pace and skills to beat opponents, but they also need to think clearly so that they can decide when to try and run and when to pass or kick instead.

SPEED AND RUNNING LINES

Running with the ball can sometimes seem the simplest thing in the world, especially when an excellent attacking move puts you into large amounts of space with no opponents to worry about. Much of the time, however, you will run knowing that defenders lie just ahead ready to tackle you. Players who have great pace have an advantage, of course, but even the fastest runners need more than speed to beat opponents regularly.

This ball carrier is running with the ball held in both hands in front of him at around chest height. His head is up and he is scanning the pitch around and in front of him helping him to calculate his next move. Behind and to the side, a team-mate is sprinting in support in order to receive a pass.

One vital technique is to choose a good running line. This is the angle and direction which you make your run. A successful running line might surprise opponents, allowing you to burst through their defence. Out in the open, a player may change his running line to veer away from opponents in the distance. Alternatively, a player could move a little closer towards his own team-mates so that he has support and is not isolated.

1 A sidestep is a sudden change of direction that can leave a defender unable to put in a tackle. This ball carrier veers to his left. He intends to sidestep to his right to pass the defender.

2 As the ball carrier approaches the defender, he plants his left foot and drives powerfully off it at a sharp angle. He shifts his weight to his right foot quickly and leans away from the defender.

3 The defender is surprised by the sudden change of direction. He is unbalanced and unable to tackle the ball carrier.

EVASIVE MOVES

Changes of speed and direction are evasive moves that can help you beat an opponent. Changes of direction include the sidestep move (see above) and the swerve, where having leaned in one direction, you take a step across your body and lean away to veer around an opponent. A change of speed can confuse defenders who have to predict where they must head to make a tackle. By slowing down dramatically, you may make them hesitate and change their own speed and direction, giving you enough time and space to suddenly sprint away.

1 A dummy will work only when you have support nearby making the defender unsure who to tackle. Here, two attackers run at a defender.

2 The ball carrier starts to swing his arms across his body as if he is about to pass. The defender believes the pass is about to happen and moves towards the receiver to make a tackle.

3 At the last moment and with the defender committed to heading to his right, the ball carrier draws the ball back into his chest sharply as he angles his run to the defender's left.

4 The defender is on the wrong foot and does not have enough time to react and make a tackle. The ball carrier sprints away hard keeping his head up in order to judge his next move.

ATTACKING

Attacking is all about finding space and getting past the other team's defence. While a piece of individual brilliance can unlock an opposition defence, most attacks involve a number of players working together slickly and accurately.

DID YOU KNOW?

South Africa's Morné Steyn was the leading points scorer at the 2011 Ruby World Cup with 62 points.

BREAKS AND SUPPORT

Teams practise making fast, accurate passes, running good attacking lines and attacking moves, such as the dummy pass and the scissors (see page 19) to get a player with the ball to break through a defensive line. Once through, the player needs support from his team-mates. Support players need to sprint hard to get within passing distance of their team-mate. This will allow him to make a pass or throw a dummy to beat another opponent in his way. An isolated player with the ball is vulnerable because, once tackled, he has to release the ball and is likely to give away possession.

Pass out of tackle

1 To take advantage of a team-mate in support nearby, the player with the ball tries to keep the ball alive as he is tackled.

2 The tackled player tries to stay on his feet as long as possible. He raises his arms to keep them out of the tackler's grasp while his team-mate arrives.

3 Twisting his body, the tackled player manages to make a pass for his team-mate to collect.

GAPS AND MISMATCHES

Attacking players may look for a rapid thrust through the opposition defence but if one does not occur, they must stay patient. A series of passes and runs can keep possession going and tie up defenders in other parts of the pitch. This can lead to gaps appearing and a good pass can release an attacker into one of these. Possession can also lead to a mismatch, for example, where a fast winger finds himself up against a slower forward. A good series of passes by one team can sometimes lead to an overlap – where the attacking team has more players in a part of the pitch than there are defenders.

Overlap

1 The attacking team has an overlap with three players against two defenders. Excellent running and timing are still required to take advantage of this opportunity.

2 The player with the ball times his pass so that one defender is committed to tackling him. His pass to the right releases his team-mate into space.

3 The player with the ball shows superb timing to release the crucial pass to his team-mate on the overlap. He must get the ball away before the defender opposite him can make the tackle.

4 The overlapping player now sprints away in space. His team-mates follow to offer support farther up the pitch.

Scissors pass

A scissors pass sees the ball carrier make a sudden change of direction to run diagonally. A team-mate suddenly shifts his running line to run an opposite diagonal line behind the ball carrier. The aim is to trick defenders into following the original ball carrier. As the players cross, the ball carrier twists and makes a short pass to his team-mate. This sudden change in direction can unbalance defenders.

Attacking players can also fake a scissors move. This is called a dummy scissors. The player with the ball twists sharply to pass to his team-mate. At the last moment, though, the player withdraws the ball into his body and continues running.

TACKLING

Tackling is a vital part of the game and one that must be practised regularly and intensely so that you can make a safe and secure tackle in the heat of a game. A failed tackle not only lets the player with the ball get free, but also, with you stranded on the ground, it means that your side is a player short.

TACKLING TRAINING

Tackling can seem daunting at first, but, if practised well under the eye of your coach, you will build up confidence and skill. A coach will walk you through your early tackling attempts, sometimes using padded crash mats and tackle bags. You will then build up speed and intensity over a number of sessions.

Players should learn to tackle from both sides using their left and their right shoulders and to make tackles from the side and from the front.

Tap tackle

A tap tackle is a last-ditch tackle when an opponent with the ball is almost past you. The tackler uses his hand to make a firm tap on his opponent's foot or ankle. The aim is to make the ball carrier stumble and fall. You can make a tap tackle only with your hands, never your feet.

Side-on

1 This player looks to make a side-on tackle using his right shoulder to make impact. He lines up the tackle at about waist level and drives off his left leg as his arms encircle the upper legs of his opponent.

2 The tackler drives into the ball carrier putting all his bodyweight into the tackle. He makes sure his head slips behind the hips and body of the player he is tackling. This is essential to avoid injury.

3 With his arms wrapped around his opponent's legs, the tackling player holds on firmly as both players hit the ground. A good side tackle will see you land partly on top of your opponent.

TACKLE TACTICS

Tackling is all about confidence and timing. A well-timed and targeted tackle by a smaller player will bring down a bigger player safely. A key point is to hold the player until he is fully grounded. If the tackled player falls down but is not held in the tackle he can get back to his feet and continue moving. Once tackled and on the ground, a player must release the ball and move away from it. The tackler, too, must roll away from his opponent and the ball. If either the tackler or the tackled player does not attempt to roll away, the referee will award a penalty to the opposition.

These two players launch into strong tackles using padded tackle bags. Both players wrap their arms around the tackle bags as they and the bags fall to the floor.

Front-on

1 A trickier tackle to master than the side-on tackle, the front-on tackle is a vital part of defending. Here, the tackler gets into a crouched position early with his knees bent and his right arm out as he lines up his right shoulder to receive the impact.

2 The tackler makes sure his head will be to one side of his opponent with his head up and his neck firm. The tackler shrugs his shoulder on impact and using his legs, drives his right shoulder into his opponent.

3 The tackler begins to twist as his opponent falls over his shoulder. The key here is to keep the arms tightly wrapped around the opponent's legs so that he has no option but to fall.

4 The tackler turns as his opponent falls so that he will land on his opponent's legs. The tackler looks to roll away from his opponent and to get to his feet as quickly as possible.

This referee signals a high tackle. For safety reasons, all tackles must be made no higher than the shoulder. A high tackle can be very dangerous and will often see an offender sent to the sin bin.

KEEPING POSSESSION

When players are tackled, their first thoughts must be to get into a position where their team can 'recycle' possession to keep hold of the ball and not give away a penalty. Good recycling of the ball involves excellent support play from team-mates who may form a ruck or maul.

RECYCLING AND SUPPORT

A phase of play is said to be over when a player is tackled and stopped. An attacking team looks to build a number of phases of play through good recycling of the ball to keep possession, moving forwards and hopefully finding a gap through the opposition defence and over the try line to score a try. Supporting players are vital in attacking and defending and are even more crucial in recycling. They must arrive quickly and use secure handling to keep the ball in their side's possession and not knock it on.

Presenting

1 The player with the ball has moved forwards but is about to be tackled. If there was a player in close support, he might consider passing the ball out of the tackle before he has fallen.

2 As the ball carrier is tackled and falls, he turns so that he is facing back to his own try line. He must release the ball as soon as he is on the ground and places the ball back with his arm.

3 A team-mate in support has reacted quickly and arrives. Staying on his feet he gets low and, keeping his eyes on the ball, gathers it securely.

4 The support player can now sprint away to continue his side's attack. The tackled player should look to get up as quickly as possible as he may be needed as a support player later.

RUCKS

When a tackled player is grounded, he must release the ball. A ruck occurs in this situation when one or more players from each side are on their feet and in contact above the ball on the floor. Players from each team try to drive over the ball to win possession. If the ball is not played out of a ruck quickly enough, the referee will award a scrum. The laws surrounding rucks are among the game's most complex, but your coach will be able to demonstrate them with practical examples so that you understand.

A player is tackled by two opponents and falls to the ground, releasing the ball. Three team-mates are in support and will look to form a ruck and drive over the ball. The rucking players drive forwards with a low body position but with their shoulders above their hips.

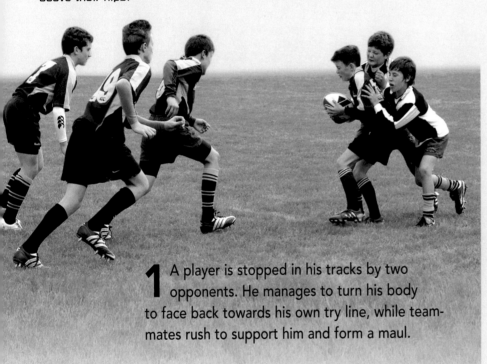

1 A player is stopped in his tracks by two opponents. He manages to turn his body to face back towards his own try line, while team-mates rush to support him and form a maul.

2 The ball carrier's team-mates join the maul with their shoulders higher than their hips.

3 The attacking players manage to drive forwards with all players still standing.

4 The incoming player has not joined the maul, but is taking the ball off the ball carrier instead.

MAULS

A maul shares some similarities with the ruck, but forms when a player is tackled and manages to stay on his or her feet and at least one player from each side is in contact around the tackled player. Further players can join the maul providing they follow the laws. A maul can be hard to stop once it is moving forwards. If the maul does stop moving, however, a referee will usually tell the players that they have five seconds to get the ball out of the maul or the other team will be awarded a scrum.

LINEOUTS

The lineout is a way of restarting play when the ball has left the pitch over the touchlines. Equal numbers of players from each side line up in rows standing a minimum of 5 metres (17 feet) in from the pitch. These players jump for the ball when it is thrown in.

LINEOUT LAWS

The team who did not touch the ball last before it crossed the touchline is awarded the throw-in. The one exception is where a team has a penalty and kicked it straight into touch. In this situation, the kicking team gets the throw.

The lineout involves two rows of between two and seven forwards. All players not in the lineout must stand at least 10 metres (33 feet) away. The scrum-half is part of the lineout and can stand closer, but not in the rows of players, which must have a 1-metre (3 $\frac{1}{3}$-feet) gap between them. Lifting is not allowed at junior level, but lineout players can be lifted by team-mates in matches for older age groups and adult rugby.

Much of the responsibility for a lineout's success lies with the throwing-in team's hooker. He must throw straight and at the perfect height and distance for his lineout jumpers to catch the ball.

lineout forwards

This full lineout has seven players from one side in a line awaiting their hooker's throw. The scrum-half stands behind them waiting for a tap down or pass. Two of the players are crouched and ready to help protect their jumping team-mates.

scrum-half

24

There are a number of throwing techniques used. Here, the hooker grips the ball with his throwing hand at the back of the ball and his other hand to the side and front to offer support.

LINEOUT TACTICS

Sides with a stronger lineout than the opposition may often kick to touch and look to steal the ball at the other team's lineout. Sometimes, to counter this, struggling teams reduce the number of players in a lineout to the bare minimum of two forwards or try a different lineout move. Lineout moves are worked on in training and are often given code names so that the hooker, scrum-half and the lineout jumpers will know where the ball will be thrown.

Lineout

1 The hooker stands with his feet behind the sideline and lines up his throw carefully. He must carefully judge the height and distance of his throw.

2 With his shoulders and body parallel to the sideline, the hooker takes his arms back to throw the ball.

3 The hooker's hands move forwards into the throw. He follows through with his arms and hands after releasing the ball and can now step back onto the pitch.

The opposing team is allowed to contest the lineout. Here, a jumper from the non-throwing team has anticipated where the ball will head and has timed his jump to steal the ball. As he lands, he sends a good pass back to his scrum-half.

The jumpers in a lineout can either catch the ball or tap it back to their scrum-half. Here, the jumper has secured the ball and makes a quick two-handed pass back to his scrum-half.

Here, the jumper catches the ball using two hands and, as he lands, his team-mates in the lineout move around him to establish a maul. The 'catch-and-drive' move close to your opponent's try line can lead to a good try-scoring chance.

SCRUMS

Scrums are used for restarting play in a number of situations. These include when the ball has been passed forwards, when the ball has been knocked on and when the ball has not come out of a maul or a ruck. A team can also choose to play a scrum when it is awarded a penalty.

A front row practises its technique using a scrummaging machine. The coach will concentrate on the players maintaining a good, safe body position with a flat back and bent legs. Scrummaging techniques should only ever be practised with an experienced coach in attendance.

SCRUM FORMATION

In junior versions of the game, scrums may have three or five players a side. In the full version of the game, a scrum usually consists of the eight forwards from each team. They bind together as a unit of eight and, on the referee's instructions, the front rows of each side engage, forming a tunnel down the middle of the scrum. The scrum-half rolls the ball down this tunnel where the hooker hooks it back with his foot. The ball should travel to the back of the scrum where the number eight has the responsibility of controlling it.

This is how the players line up for an eight-a-side scrum. The front row consists of the two prop forwards who stand either side of the hooker. The two second row or lock forwards bind together tightly and place their heads between the hooker and the props. The flankers bind onto each side of the scrum, while at the back is the number eight who puts his head between the two second row forwards. All players must stay bound together until the scrum has ended.

number eight

prop forward

hooker

prop forward

lock forward

lock forward

flanker

flanker

1 The scrum-half feeds the scrum by rolling the ball into the middle. The ball must be rolled straight or the referee will award a free kick to the opposition.

2 The hooker uses his boot to strike at the ball and roll it back. Both hookers are the only players allowed to raise their feet in the scrum.

3 The ball is controlled at the back of the scrum by the number eight. Once the ball is out, the scrum is over.

4 This scrum-half comes in bent low to gather the ball at the feet of his number eight. He fires off a sharp pass to one of his backs.

NEXT MOVE

Once the ball is at the back of a scrum and under the control of the number eight, players have a number of options as to what they do next. The number eight can pick the ball up and pass it or run with the ball. Alternatively, the whole scrum can try to drive forwards to gain valuable territory. The most common move is for the scrum-half to collect the ball and either kick or pass the ball to a team-mate.

While practising using a scrum machine, the number eight at the back of the scrum picks up the ball and drives forwards powerfully with the ball in his hands.

SCRUM SAFETY

The scrum is one of the most dangerous areas of the game and players should always follow a referee's or coach's instructions. They should never practise the scrum alone without a coach.

27

GOAL AND DROP KICKING

There are three situations where a kick can result in points. Penalties and conversions are kicks made with the ball static on the ground or sitting on a kicking tee. Drop kicks are attempts during open play where the ball is dropped out of the hands and kicked on the half-volley.

A plastic kicking tee holds the ball in place when a kicker attempts a penalty kick on goal or a conversion. This kicker is lining up the ball carefully on the kicking tee.

PLACE KICKING

Place kicking is where the ball is placed on the ground in a divot of turf, on a mound of sand or perched on a kicking tee. Place kicking is used for penalty kicks on goal (worth three points) and when taking a conversion kick (worth two points) after a try is scored. A conversion kick is taken in line with where the try was scored. Successful place kicking relies on plenty of practice so that the kicking action is accurate. A team with a strong kicker has an excellent chance of turning penalties into points to win a game.

Here, you can see how the goal kicker has planted his standing foot a short distance to the side of the ball and a little behind so that only his toes are in line with the ball.

Place kicking

1 This player is using the 'round the corner' method of kicking for goal. He has taken a number of paces back and to the side to be at an angle to the ball.

2 The player approaches the ball with his head down and eyes on the ball. He plants his non-kicking foot to the side of the ball and a little behind it.

3 With his body weight on his standing foot, his kicking leg swings through. His boot makes contact to send the ball over the crossbar.

2 The player lets go of the ball, dropping it downwards. At the same time, his kicking foot starts to swing through. He keeps his head down and his body weight is on his standing foot.

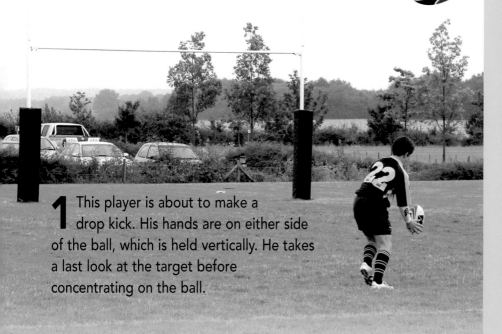

1 This player is about to make a drop kick. His hands are on either side of the ball, which is held vertically. He takes a last look at the target before concentrating on the ball.

3 Using his arms to help balance, the player swings his kicking leg forwards. The ball drops almost alongside his standing foot. The player times the swing of his leg so that his boot connects just after the ball bounces.

DROP KICKS

Drop kicks are kicks out of hand that are aimed at goal. If they sail over successfully they are worth three points. They often occur when a team has the ball close to the other team's try line but cannot find a way through. In this situation, a kicker may drop back a distance to attempt a drop kick.

The whole drop kick action must be performed smoothly but rapidly, as any hesitation increases the risk of the ball being charged down by an opponent. The basic drop kick technique is also used in other situations such as kick-off and restarting play from a 22-metre drop out. In these situations, the kicker has time and may choose to hit the ball higher so that his team has enough time to run up and challenge the opposition.

Drop Kick

4 The ball rises high into the air. The player's kicking foot swings through to complete a high follow-through.

GLOSSARY AND RESOURCES

Glossary

backs The group of seven players in a team who usually line up behind the forwards and are involved in attacking play.

charge down Blocking an opponent's kick with your hands, arms or body.

conversion A kick for goal awarded after a try is scored which, if taken successfully, is worth two points.

drop kick A kick where the ball is dropped to the ground and kicked just as it bounces.

dummy A technique where a player pretends to pass the ball to deceive a defender.

forwards The group of eight players in a team who are usually involved in the scrums and lineouts.

grubber kick A type of kick which sends the ball bouncing end over end along the ground.

knock-on When the ball touches the hand or arm of a player and moves forwards and touches the ground as a result.

lineout The usual way of restarting play after the ball has gone out of play over the touchlines. Two equal numbers of players from both sides line up in rows and one player throws the ball in.

maul A formation of players brought around a ball carrier who is still in possession of the ball and has not been brought to the ground.

overlap An attacking sequence which results in attackers outnumbering defenders.

penalty kick A kick awarded to one team when the other side has broken one of the laws of the game.

place kick A kicking technique where the ball is placed on the ground before being kicked.

possession Having the ball under control.

recycle Maintaining and using possession after making contact with the opposition.

ruck A loose formation of players created around a free ball or a player who has been tackled to the ground with the ball.

scrum A method of restarting a game where the forwards from both teams bind together and pack down. The scrum-half feeds the ball in and the hooker strikes the ball to the number eight's feet at the back of the scrum.

sidestep A sudden change of sideways direction used by the ball carrier to get past a defender.

sin bin When a player has committed a serious offence, he or she is sent to the sin bin. The referee shows the player a yellow card and sends him or her off the pitch for 10 minutes.

tap tackle A firm tap of an opponent's ankles by a defender's hand.

tag rugby A non-contact form of the game where players 'tackle' each other by pulling off tags that are fixed to their kit.

try A method of scoring by touching the ball down in the opponent's in-goal area. A try is worth five points.

Diet and nutrition

Top international rugby players watch their diet extremely carefully and clubs often employ expert nutritionists to monitor players. Diet is also important at junior and amateur levels.

Eating a good, balanced meal several hours or more before a match gives your body time to get energy from the meal. A balanced diet contains a combination of the three main food groups – carbohydrates, proteins and fats.

Complex carbohydrates are especially good for providing energy for performance. They are found in foods such as pasta, fruit and vegetables. These foods are major features of a professional rugby player's diet.

Proteins are important in building muscle strength and stamina. Protein can be found in lean meat, such as chicken, and pulses, such as beans.

www.mypyramid.gov/kids/index.html
Healthy eating is sometimes shown as a food pyramid. This webpage from the US Department of Agriculture provides lots of downloadable files and posters

Resources

http://www.irb.com/index.html
The homepage of the International Rugby Board, the organisation which runs world rugby. Here, you can download the latest laws of the game and read about tournaments, world rankings and lots more.

http://www.rfu.com/index.cfm/fuseaction/
rfuhome.community_detail/storyid/5972
The section of the English Rugby Football Union's website devoted to women's rugby with news of coaching, competition and clubs.

http://www.planet-rugby.com/
An international website with coverage of leagues, cups and national teams from all over the world.

http://www.irishrugby.ie/
This official website for Irish rugby offers a large collection of skills, tips and drills, as well as the laws of mini and tag rugby under its coaching and development pages, which can be viewed for free.

http://aru.rugby.com.au/onlinecoaching
The online coaching pages at the Australian Rugby Union's website are full of lessons, drills and tips for junior rugby players.

http://www.rugbydir.com/index.php
A growing collection of great links to rugby websites for coaching, tournaments and specific rugby clubs and teams.

http://sportsvl.com/ball/rugby/rugbyunion.htm
A huge collection of links to rugby union websites including player and club pages.

INDEX